Flex

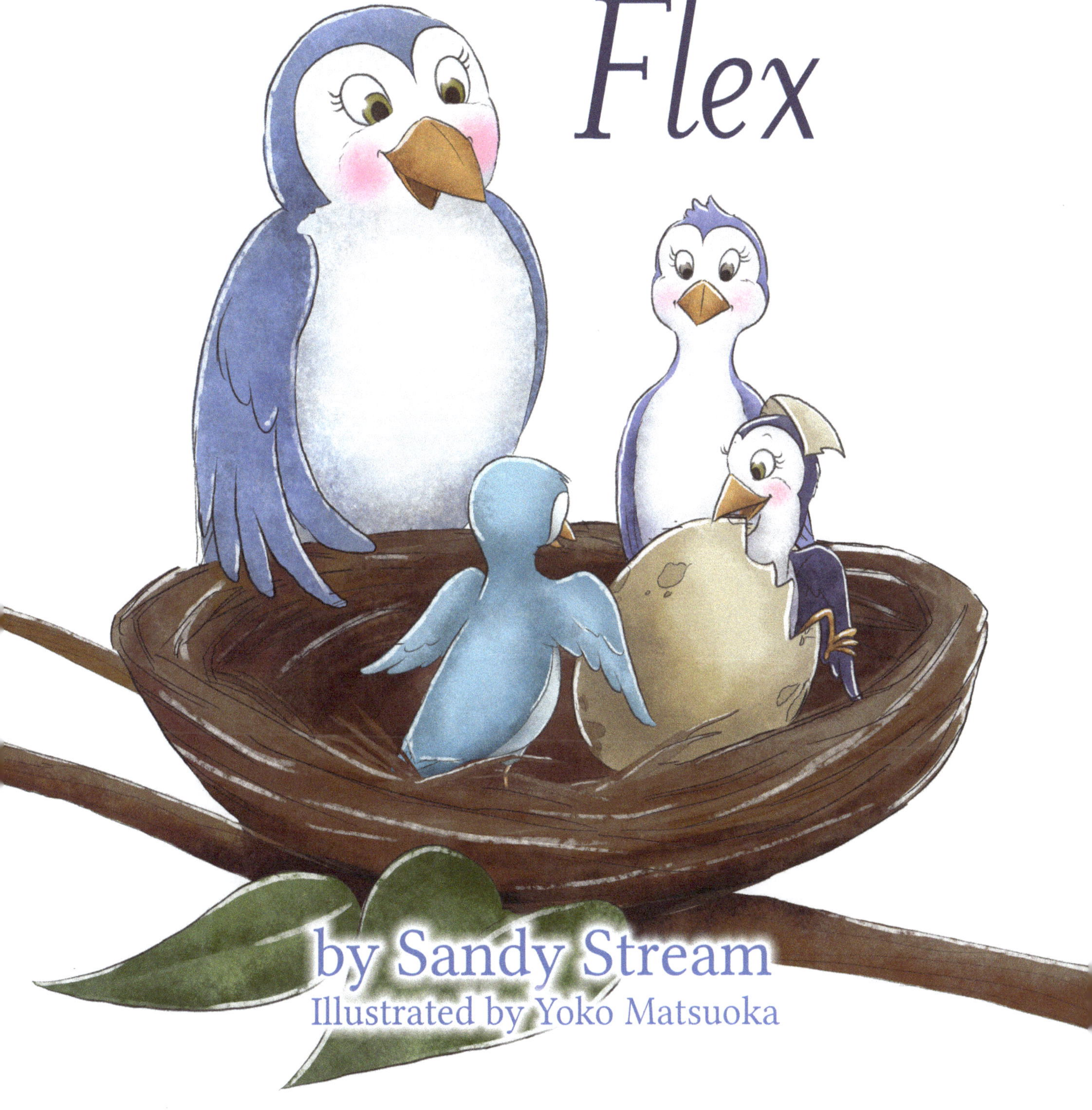

by Sandy Stream
Illustrated by Yoko Matsuoka

Flex. By Sandy Stream
Illustrated by Yoko Matsuoka
Edited by Tomoko Matsuoka

ISBN 978-0-9739481-8-9

Copyright © 2014 by Sandy Stream Publishing. Montreal, Canada.
All rights reserved. No part of this book may be reproduced, stored in a retrieval system, or transmitted in any form or by any means without the written permission of Sandy Stream Publishing.

On a Personal Note

Is it possible to lose ourselves completely? To cover up our essence so well that it is no longer able to shine?

We often avoid being ourselves in order to survive in this world. It takes courage to continue to respect and live in a way that is true to our essence, but I see no other way to truly be alive.

Sandy Stream

Based on *many* true stories

Once upon a time there was a nest with three little eggs.

One summer day, the first egg hatched and Sparky was born. The next day, Feathers was born. When the third egg hatched, Mama called her lovely bird "Flex" because he was so flexible when he crawled out of the little hole in his shell.

From very young, Flex wanted to fly. His mama was often flying off somewhere, so he decided to try it on his own. He spread his wings and leaped from his nest.

Nearby, a flock of young birds sat on a branch and saw that he had pink spots under his wings.

"What is that?!" chuckled one bird, pointing at the spots. The other birds laughed along as they pointed at the pink spots.

Flex hadn't known that he had spots under his wings.

Boom, boom, boom.

His heart was beating so fast.

"It's nothing!" answered Flex, quickly lowering his wings. He wanted to cry but didn't want to show it.

He felt like arrows were being shot at his chest. He was wounded and felt very weak.

From that day forward, he tried not to let anyone see his spots, or to see him fly. Whenever Flex went to the river to drink, he would close his eyes because he hated to see his reflection.

Why did I have to be born with these spots? I hate being so different. Nobody is ever going to like me like this...

Boom, boom, boom.
Flex's heart beat faster every time he passed anyone. He hated when birds looked at him.
"Look. There's Flex with the specks," they would say.
The arrows continued to fly…
Flex had so many scars from all the wounds.

As time passed, Flex's skin and feathers began to grow thicker and thicker.
The thick layer covered his body and concealed his pink spots.
It also protected him from the arrows.

Seasons passed.
Flex's coat grew thicker and harder.
His new hardened coat protected him but also concealed everything underneath—everything inside.
And his insides grew harder...
Even his heart was tougher now.
Soon, he could not feel anything at all.

Many birds were impressed, but some were afraid of Flex and his strong armor-like layer.

Flex walked around proudly with his strong coat. Whenever he passed anyone, they would move aside so as not to be knocked over by his strength.
Flex liked his strong armor.

Then one day, a storm suddenly hit, and Flex had to quickly fly to escape being hit by a falling tree.

He got cut by a branch. "Ow!" he yelped.

Boom, boom, boom, went his heart.

He was so afraid someone had seen him hurt or weak that he flew and flew and flew, far away—to the edge of the forest.

When he finally stopped, he saw an owl sitting in a tree, smiling.
The owl said, "You seem so strong, my dear friend, what are you hiding?"

Flex was surprised that the owl seemed to know about his hidden spots. This must be the wise owl everyone always spoke about.
"Owl," Flex said, "can you get rid of these ugly spots?"

The wise owl said, "Go to the ocean and you shall see that the answer is in you."

Flex did as the owl said.
He built a raft and drifted on the ocean for many days. He looked at his spots but nothing happened.

He flew back to the owl and said, "I went to the ocean and looked at my spots, but they still look ugly!"

Then the owl answered, "Go back to the ocean and just look! The answer is in you."

Flex went back to his raft and thought and thought for many days.
Then he figured that maybe the owl wanted him to look inside—at his feelings.
So he closed his eyes and tried to look inside. But he couldn't see anything. It was dark.

Flex felt even *more* upset and went back to see the owl.
"I tried looking at the spots, I tried looking inside, but nothing worked! There is nothing there!"
The owl asked, "What do you think the stars see when they look down at you?"

Flex went back to the ocean and got on the raft. He looked up and saw the stars. He hadn't noticed them all this time.

He imagined he was a star looking down and looked at himself through the stars' eyes.

He saw the armor he had created—to protect himself—reflecting in the moonlight as if it were made out of metal. Flex finally understood why he could not see what was going on inside.

He went back to Owl and said,
"Can you help me see what is happening inside? How can I see through this armor?"
The owl said, "Can you still feel the ocean?"

He went back on the raft and closed his eyes.
He felt the waves underneath him.
He let his body move in rhythm with the waves of the ocean and his breath move with the wind.

He let the ocean move him—move him inside...
He felt nauseous and let it continue.
His insides started to sway and move, and he became even more nauseous and very weak...

Boom, boom, boom. His heart started beating quickly. His body started to shake and shiver. Then he started feeling everything—everything he hadn't felt all this time. He was so very weak...
He felt all the arrows and all the wounds. He felt like he was bleeding inside. He coughed and coughed and threw up all his pain...

Then he let out a long and powerful howl, like an injured wolf, into the sky. He cried to the moon all night long.
The metal-like armor began to crack from all the movement...

The armor broke into pieces and fell, bit by bit, into the ocean...
Flex's chest opened up, and he had more space to breathe. His body used the space to adjust itself and became soft and flexible again.

Then he looked in the water and saw the stars lighting up his reflection.
Now he could see the stars in all their beauty. Each one was different from the other, yet each was shining.

In the morning, the sun rose.
He felt it penetrate his flexible and exposed skin. He opened his chest and breathed in the light. His heart had space to expand—and to soften.
He was able to feel again…feel everything inside himself and everything in the world around him.

Suddenly he heard a cry...
He turned around and saw a little turtle struggling in the water. He flew over and helped the turtle back to shore.

"Thank you!" said the relieved turtle.
Flex smiled.

Flex lifted his wings, spread them to their full width, and flew back to join his world.

The now

The River Series

Sparky Can Fly
Sparky's Mama
Tweets and Hurricanes
Feathers
Flex
Roots
The River

www.RiverSpeaks.com